Windows 10:

2019 User Manual. Learn Everything You Need to Know About Windows 10

CONTENTS

Thank you for purchasing this book!

We always try to give more value then you expect. That's why we've updated the content and you can get it for FREE. You can get the digital version for free because you bought the print version.

The book is under the match program from Amazon. You can find how to do this using next URL: https://www.amazon.com/gp/digital/ep-landing-page

I hope it will be useful for you.

Introduction

When it comes to using Windows, Windows 10 is the newest and most marvelous new system for you to try out.

How do you get started with it? You might have never tried this system, nor have you truly used it before. Well, you're about to find out, for this book will be a comprehensive guide to truly understanding Windows 10,

In this, you will get the full slew of various benefits that can be had by switching to Windows 10, along with how to do some of the core features that you need. It is also of note that you can from this as well, learn how to truly navigate a computer, so if you have never done it before, this is honestly how you do it. We will take you from the bottom to the top, the beginning to the advanced level, and by the end of this, you will truly be able to understand Windows 10 in the ways that you want to.

So, what are you waiting for? It's time for you to truly use this system to your advantage, start engaging in the benefits of

Windows 10, make use of it in your life, and truly make it so that you're able to get the results that you need from this. Use it today, and get what you want from it, and it will help you make the most out of this now, and to truly make it so that you're getting what you want now and in the future.

Chapter 1 – Introduction to Windows 10

Windows 10 is a great upgrade, and worth the money. But, what are some of the new features? What are some of the requirements for it? Well, you're about to find out, for this chapter will give you a basic overview of Windows 10

New Windows 10 features

There are many new features to Windows 10, and here are just a few of the ones that you can get the moment that you upgrade:

-   New 3D photo effects for your photos

-   A filed start menu where the applications are on files in a neat fashion

- Cortana, which is Microsoft's answer to a digital assistant, allowing you to have a personal digital assistant right at your disposal

- The Edge Browser, which is essentially an upgraded Internet Explorer. You can disable this as well, which is really just there for legacy purposes. But, the fact that you can get rid of it this time around does make a huge difference.

- Victual desktops, which allow you to go back and forth between having open apps, or multiple desktops

- The action center, which tells you all of your notifications and the like

- Revamped Mail and Calendar apps, which are much better. They are faster, more responsive, fit more info into an area, it will allow you to gesture controls to your inbox with just a few swipes, and it is configurable as well, fitting both tablets and PCs

- The Xbox app which will allow you to actually stream on Twitch, see your friends, select options to view your clips, create a party, send an IM, and a lot of other features. You can stream games with your PC alone, making streaming a whole lot easier.

- The continuum feature which allows you to switch the interfaces between the PC desktop and the Windows-8 if you feel like it's better suited for you. A nice hybrid action can help you with using it effectively.

- Windows ink which allows you to add new inking apps to use with your stylus. You can use the stylus for your apps, making it a lot easier to write if you are using a tablet.

All of these and so much more are some of the new features to Windows 10, and they can make a world of a difference for those looking to upgrade at this point.

How to Upgrade to Windows 10

Now, there was a free upgrade for this, but it ended back in July of 2016. Either if you want to upgrade to Windows 10, you can do so by buying it from the website, downloading it to the computer directly, or if you have a computer with a small amount of space, you want to put it onto a USB drive. From there, you can launch it, and follow the prompts.

The upgrade could have been done if you did start the upgrade and reach the welcome screen before the date, but usually, if you do not have this already, you will have to buy it.

If you have Windows 10, you can reinstall it or do a clean install on the device that it was on. The nice thing about it is that you will not need a product key to activate this if it is on the same hardware, so if you have to do a clean sweep, you can still do it with this. You should check out the download website in order to get the data.

Now, the time that it takes for this upgrade to happen does depend on your device and how you configure it. If you got a brand-new computer, chances are it's already on there, and it will take about an hour. If your computer is older, it might end up taking lover for you to get this upgrade. Typically, if your computer is newer and performs higher, it does upgrade faster as well.

Computer Requirements for This

With Windows 10, you need to follow a few of the hardware requirements. It is worth adding to your computer if you do not have it already, and if you do have it, make sure that they are on par with what's listed here.

For the processor, you need something that is 1 GHz or faster than that. You need at least one gig of memory ideally for the 32-bit, or if you go 64-bit, you will need two gigs of this.

For the disk space, you need about 16 GB for ideal running.

If you do not have it already, get a graphics card that is either Microsoft DirectX 9 or a WDDM driver.

Finally, you need a Microsoft account and access to the internet for full installation.

Now, if you need to free up space for the upgrade, such as in the example of devices that have 32 GB on them or older, and you might need some additional space. If you are struggling with this, try to remove files and apps that you do not need, or run the disk cleanup to get some space put in.

During this upgrade, if you are asked to free up space on the device, you will need to do so. You can however also put an external drive on there, but if you do attach it, you need to keep it in a place that is safe once you are done upgrading in the off chance that you need to recover something from the device.

Chapter 2 – Setting Up and maintaining Windows 10

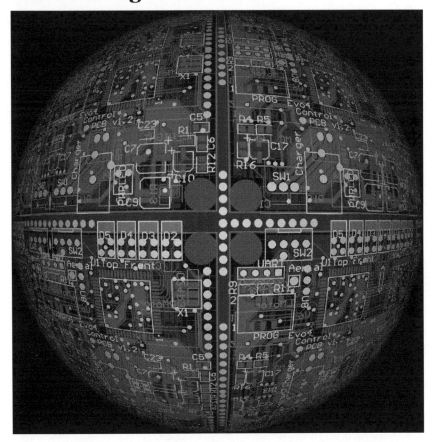

Putting together Windows 10 is actually simple, and there are a few things that you can make your experience the best. Here are but a few of the great ways to set up and maintain Windows 10.

Settings to configure

There are a few settings that you should configure before you get started with Windows 10, and here they are.

The first is stopping automatic Windows 10 updates. You should make sure that the automatic restart is stopped. To do this, go to the start menu, and choose the advanced update, and then Advanced Windows Update options. From this, you want to change the settings to notify schedule restart. This, in turn, will let you know when it is time to restart.

Also, disable key logger. This is what Windows 1- will observe what you are typing. It is supposed to help make it better, but it can be a bit weird to have. To fix this, you should go to settings, privacy settings, general, and then disable the option to send Microsoft how you write, and also make sure to select the option in the speech, inking and typing area that and turn that off as well.

You should as well make sure that Windows 10 stops sending bandwidth updates to others, and while this might seem like a good idea, it is sharing information with others. You should go to settings, then update and security, go to the Windows update on the left side, and choose advanced options. From there, you want to go to choose how updates are delivered, and then switch it to off.

Finally, disable Wi-Fi sense, which is where Microsoft sends the password to those Facebook and Skype friends. It is easy to switch off. You need to go to the start menu, go to Wi-Fi settings, and then choose to change this. Manage it, and make sure that you do not share these with anyone who does not need them.

Appearance and personalization

There are the appearances and personalization tab, which allows you to change many of the wild settings on the Windows 10 system.

Personalization: this is where the screensaver, themes, and ways to save the window screen as a theme. It essentially allows you to choose what it looks like on screen.

The display lets you mess with the screen, such as the resolution and the connection to computer screens.

Taskbar and navigation: this adds program shortcuts and to help you remove them as well.

Ease of access: this is used to make it easier to navigate if you are blind.

File explorer: this tweaks the behavior of folders

Fonts: allows you to look at the fonts that you have

You can use any of these to further personalize your Windows 10 system to the best that it can be.

Setting up the Screensaver

You might love the generic Windows 10 screensaver that is there, but if you do not want to have it like that, or you want to create a slideshow, it is easy to do.

Now first, you could go to control panel and choose appearances and themes, and from there go to what you want to get. On the other hand, you can just go to the search bar and type in the screensaver. Press enter, and then choose the downward arrow and select a screensaver that you have.

Now, you can preview this to make sure it looks good before you decide on this. You should look at the screensaver options too.

If you want to, you can also add security by choosing the display logon screen checkbox, and by checking it, it will prevent people from using your computer when you are not there. This will ask for a password when waking up, or with a screensaver. Obviously, this is optional.

When done, press OK.

That is all there is to it. It is simple to add a nice screensaver and theme to your device.

Sound and connecting Equipment along with Bluetooth

Adding sound and other devices to your computer can help improve the audio quality of it. But, how do you do it? We are going to first go over how you can do it with speakers that are wired, and how to do it with the speakers that are Bluetooth, or even headphones as well.

Now, you want to right click on the speaker icon in the right corner and choose the option that says Playback devices.

You will see the window, and from there, you can click the speaker that you want it to connect to. You can test it by pressing the test button to see if it works.

Now, for Configuring, you should make sure that the device has a green checkmark since that is where the sound will be coming from.

You can then test, adjust as needed, and go from there.

For Bluetooth, you will first want to turn on whatever device you have so that the computer can find it.

Then, go to the Bluetooth icon on your PC. Check this and turn it on. If you have not yet, go to the action center and choose the option that says Bluetooth.

Find the device name, and then choose to connect it.

If you need to pair them up, do so, but usually, once it's connected, you can then turn them on and off, and you are good. To disconnect, you can simply turn off the Bluetooth function.

For a mouse or keyboard, it is a bit different, but virtually the same thing.

First, you got to turn it on and make sure it's seen. From there, go to settings, choose devices, and then choose Bluetooth and other devices.

You should turn on Bluetooth, and then choose to add Bluetooth or other devices, and then follow the instructions to connect it. From there, you are done.

Removing Programs

Sometimes you have programs that you just do not want on there. Fortunately, there are ways to remove.

To remove a program, go to control panel, and from there, you should go to programs, programs and features, and then choose this. If you need to repair, you can, otherwise, you can remove the program by choosing to uninstall the program. You simply follow the directions on the screen to do this.

Backing Up Data with File History

Windows 10 makes it easy for you to back up your data. How this works, is that it will take snapshots of these files, and store them in a hard drive that is external. Over time, it will build a vast library of various versions of docs that you can recover, or the like. Now, you can go dip into this and literally copy sentences from previous documents.

So how does this all work exactly? Well to get there, you can go to the settings version, update & security, and from there go to thy backup. Once there, you can then put the external hard drive into there.

You can then go to settings, and press the plus sign next to add a drive. You will then choose the external to connect to, and that is that. The file history will proceed to archive your data.

You will also see a slider that says, "Automatically back up my files" and you should leave this one. That way is everything automatically backed up.

It will automatically back up various files in your User folder, but to add other folders, you can go to more options, and choose from which files you want it to back up. You can then press the plugins to add this to it, and to remove, you can scroll down, highlight, and then remove this.

This will allow you to help keep everything backed up in case if things go sour.

Access to Folders from Other Computers

Now, if you want to access folders that are present on other computers, the easiest, and most retrievable is to use OneDrive.

OneDrive is the cloud storage system for Microsoft devices. To use this, sign into your account on the computer that you have, you can then add files to your OneDrive system, and from there, if you are on another computer, you can then log in, and you will be able to access this completely. It is a great system.

For those of us who are looking to manage the various aspects of Windows 10, this is how, and it certainly can make a world of a difference.

Chapter 3 – The Start Menu

Your first location on Windows 10 is the start menu. This is where most of the apps are located, and we will go over each of them. What they entail, and some important stuff about your accounts as well.

Windows Welcome

When you first open this, you will immediately be hit with the welcome screen. This is something that you see after you press the middle button to go to the desktop. This might require a password if you are on a computer that has a password protection on it.

You can do some things with it. To get rid of the start screen, you want to go to settings, choose personalization, select the start section, and turn off the Use Start full screen choice. From there, it might also require you to turn off other applications as well, so keep that in mind.

User Accounts

User accounts are the accounts that you want to have that will showcase whose desktop is whose. This is important to have if you are using Windows 10 on a computer that has many users, such as a family computer. If you do not want children getting into your Microsoft account, you will want to consider adding user accounts to your Windows 10 system.

The first thing that you do is you go to the Windows icon at the bottom, choose settings, press the button that says Accounts on it with the person on it, and from there, you can go to Family & Other Users. Click on that, and then press "Add someone else to this PC." Now, you should then press the top option that says you do not have the person's information to sign in. From there, you want to "Add a User without a Microsoft Account." If you do have someone that already has one, you will want to go back, have them sign in, and voila.

They can then put in their name and password, choose the Next option, and then press the Windows icon on there. You want to go to the user icon that is in the upper left area when you open up the menu in Start. Choose the user, and then have them sign in to the account.

To switch users, you literally go to switching the user on the device and then add in the login details. This is great to have and makes it easier.

Your Microsoft Account

So, what is a Microsoft account? Well, a Microsoft account is how you connect Outlook, Hotmail, Office 365, Skype, Xbox, or Windows together. If you want to take advantage of the OneDrive cloud storage system on other computers, you will need a Microsoft account. They are easy and free with a valid email address or phone number.

This account will give you access to games and apps from the store as well, and it will let you see your settings on various devices as well.

To get one of these, you go to account.microsfot.com for best results.

To sign into this, you can push the start button, then go to settings, choose accounts, and then email & app accounts. You can from there, in the "Accounts used by other app" choose top "Add a Microsoft account." You will need to from here add in your login credentials and verify your account by putting a confirmation code into there. From there, you should be signed in, and you can manage these accounts as well by choosing the user and logging in to that account as well.

How to Password Protect your Account

For some people, having a password on there is imperative, since there might be sensitive information on there. Passwords might not be used if you are the only person on this computer, or if you trust someone enough that they will not go through it. But, how do you put a password in? How do you change it if you feel that this information might be compromised? Well, you are about to find out.

The first thing that you should to do is to go to accounts from the settings area in the start menu. You want to go to sign-in options on there. If you see the password area, you can choose to add a new password. If you already have a password and need to change it, you can press the Change button under it to change the password itself.

Now, if you do want to change this, you need to sign in with the current password. You will be able to do that, and from here, there will be a confirmation code given to you from your mobile device. Change it, and from there, you will have to enter the old password again, and then add in the new one, and reenter it once more. From there, you press the enter button.

If you have a screen that tells you that you have done it, then congrats, you have!

There is also the option of changing it to a pin, and here is how you do that. Do the same steps as before, but instead of changing the password, change it to a pin. You need to re-enter your password, and then put the pin in. enter it once again and then press OK. You should be able to log into everything with the pin itself from here.

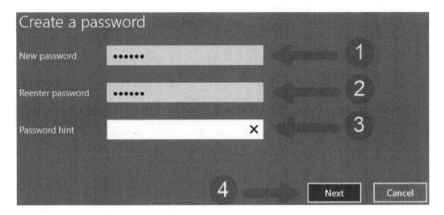

New updates to the Start Menu

There are new updates to the start menu, which are nice and do help make it much more organized. Here are just a few of the major features added.

First, the menus are in the start folder. These allow you to make the menu personalized. You can create a panel, which drops down that shows everything inside, including social media apps.

You can drag and drop each of these as well in order to navigate this.

The tab preview area in the Edge browser also tells you about the tabs that you have open. You can scroll through horizontally to look at the thumbnail, with the preview bar dropping down.

Then there is the Edge jumplist. If you want to put in a new window on Edge, you literally can right-click the Edge icon on the taskbar as well, making it easy to put it directly onto what you want.

With the start menu as well, you can go through the various apps that you have, pin them there as well, and organize them into folders. This, in turn, will make your ability to navigate it all the easier.

With the start menu, it's made everything a lot easier to find, and you can certainly do this immediately without having to go through too many navigation tabs. It makes this a lot easier, and it will make the overall navigation a dream.

How to Run programs and search in the Start menu

On the start menu are a whole lot of apps that you can look for. If you want to limit scrolling, you can jump to the part of the list. What you want to do, is search through this, look for the letter of the app that it begins with, and through this search, you'll be able to run it the second that you find it.

If you are still struggling with finding it, you want to use the search box, type in the name, or just push on the Windows key and type out the name of the app. This is the easiest way to search it.

You can also add or remove programs. What you want to do in order to add is to press the start button, choose all apps, and they will be represented in an alphabetical array. Right click on what you want to appear in the start menu, and then Pin to Start. Do this repeatedly until you have got all the items that you so desire. As of note, you have to do this separately, and probably the one downside to Windows 10 is that you cannot do this simultaneously.

If you are choosing from the desktop, right click the items that you want, and you can choose Pin to Start and from there it will appear. You can do this with any folder, library, file, or whatever item. Newly added parts to the start menu go on the bottom-right corner, and if you have a lot there, you will need to scroll down to look at this.

Apps you can install

Now to the extent of what kinds of apps that you can install, it really is practically endless. For example, if you want to add various Instagram stories, explore Instagram, or even edit your photos directly on your tablet or PC, you can by getting the app.

There are so many apps that you can get, such as Windows Moviemaker, Media Player Five, 8 Zip, and even Adobe. Really, the best thing to do in many of these cases is to go to the website for Microsoft apps, find the ones that you want, and then download them. For a few, you might need to pay a small fee, but it is worth it if you do like to use these apps.

Now, to add these to the start menu, it is just like the rest. You right click, choose Pin to start and from there, it will then show up on the start menu for you to see.

How to Customize the Start Menu

With the Windows 10 start menu, there are a few things that you can do in order to make it even Bette. Here are just a few of the options that you have:

You can first resize the start menu. You can drag the top Edge of this or even the right Edge of it with the mouse. If you do resize it in a horizontal manner, you can increase this by a column or icon group at one time. However, you can only do this down to one column and up to four of them.

You can also have them show more files in the columns. If you are running out of space, go to Settings>personalization>start and turn on the "show more files on start" option is there.

If you want to unpin files, you literally can right-click one of them, and then choose "unpin from start" which will take it off the start menu.

If you are running out of the room, another great option is to resize files by clicking on it with a right click, resize it and then picking the ones that you want. Four small ones fit in a medium, four medium in a large, and a wide one is one that is two medium files. So, depending on how busy your screen is, you can choose from there the file size that you want.

Finally, if you do not want the live file updates practically barking at you, it is simple to do. You right-click them, and then choose the option to "turn live file off" and that is how it's done. It is that simple.

The start menu is pretty complex, but there is a lot that you can do. This chapter highlighted just a little bit, of what is possible with this system.

Chapter 4 – The Desktop

Next, you have the desktop. This is where you typically start from, and it is where you go to various locations. The desktop is the façade where all of your programs and applications are. The start menu is the one typically at the very bottom. However, we will go into various aspects of this, how to achieve this, and other parts of it as well.

Assigning a Desktop

So how do you assign a desktop to a user? Well, it is easy really. If you do this, you will be able to put one account to a computer, so that they can have the desktop. To do this, you just have to have to do is open up the Task View pane by pressing the Task view button that is located on the taskbar. If you are confused on where that is, just press Win+Tab to get to it. From there, you can press New Desktop to add one. If you've got two of them already open, the button will appear as a gray file with a symbol of a plus sign there. You can also add one with the shortcut Win+Ctrl+D.

To switch between these, you open this up once more, and then, you can click on the one that you want to go to. But, if you press Win+Ctrl+right or left arrow, that will allow you to get to one. You can practically put unlimited desktops on there, but the pane only shows nine at once with the inability to scroll, which is one of the downsides to Windows 10.

To go from a window to one of them, you open up the Task view pane once more and choose the one that you want to go to. Once you are there, you can right-click it and remove it to the desktop that you want it on. From there, you can drag and drop Windows, which is a neat function.

Running applications from the Start menu

With Windows 10, you can change which apps you want to use. To change which ones you want, press and hold the Start button, go to Task manager and then choose the Startup function. From there, you can choose to enable or disable the app that is there. If you want to remove the app from the tab, press the Win key plus R, type in shell: startup into the run box, press Okay, and you will see the folder from there. You can then choose the app that you want to remove, and you can either press and hold, or right click it. You will want to move it to a file location, particularly the Open File Location and then press and hold, and choose to Copy. You can then put the shortcut into the folder, and there you have it, you can run it at startup.

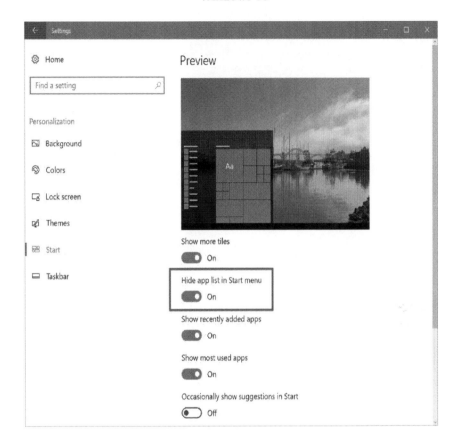

How to Change the Desktop Background

The generic Windows background looks kind of lame after a while, but there are ways to change it. Here is how you do it. From the start menu, go to settings, then personalization, and then choose a picture. You can change the accent color, the taskbar, and other items here. You can preview this to see if you like it. The background can either be a solid color a slideshow of various folder pictures.

If you go to the colors tab, you can choose the colors that you use as a background, or choose your own if you want.

Once you choose the color, you can then decide whether you should have it light or dark, depending on what is better for it.

Changing between Tablet and Desktop modes

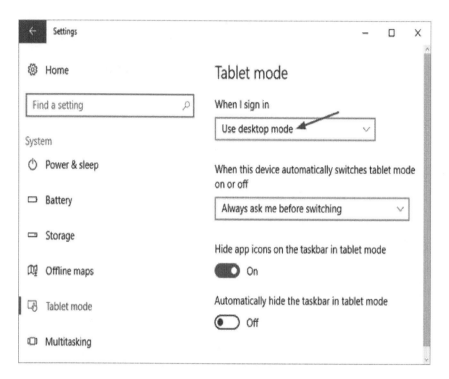

When you have a tablet, sometimes you might need to use its desktop mode, and vice versa. Tablet mode makes everything be full-screen and helps if you are using the touch function. If you have 2 in 1, you should know how to turn this off once you attach the tablet from the base, or putting it back on. It is actually super simple, and there are a couple of ways to do it.

The first is from the action center, and arguably the easiest. Press it in the taskbar, and at the bottom, choose the tablet mod to toggle it either blue or gray to turn it on and off.

To turn off and on the tablet from the settings, you should go to settings from the start menu, select system in the options, and then you will go to Tablet mode when you have a chance. You can choose at the "When I Sign" area whether you want to use desktop or tablet, whatever works for you.

These are the two best ways to do it, and ideally, the first option gives you a quick and dirty means to turn this on and off.

Trash folder

The trash folder is where all of your deleted files and such end up. Now, if you go into this, you should make sure delete it to empty it from time to time. This will free up space on your computer and make it easier for you to find this.

But, occasionally there is the problem if you do not even know where in the world it is. Well, there are easy ways to get past this. If your desktop is new and doesn't have icons at all, right click this, and select View, and if you notice that Show Desktop Icons doesn't have a checkmark, add this.

But, sometimes it is just not their period, and to fix this, you go to start, settings, personalization, themes, and then desktop icon settings. Make sure that recycle Bin is displayed there.

The recycle bin is something that you should clean out once a month. That way, it will keep your computer running well, and to a fitting state that will be helpful for you.

How to Pin apps to the Taskbar

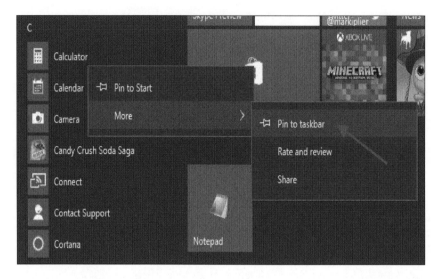

Pinning apps to the taskbar in Windows 10 is super helpful, especially if you are using them a lot. If you have certain apps that will help you get more done if they are pinned, then do that. That way, it is all right there.

To do this, you want to go to whatever app you have, whether it be the start menu or even on the desktop. Right click this, and then simply choose "pin to taskbar" and you will see it down at the bottom. This will make everything simple, and you can from here, go to wherever you need to go with the help of this app.

The notification Center

The notification center is essentially the heart of the action center in Windows 10.

Now the action center, in essence, is comprised of two sections, with the notifications that are there, and various apps that are there as well.

Notifications are generated by the system. Various developers have notifications enabled onto there, and with each, one added it could let you know what is going on, such as an update, a Windows Defender summary, or even calendar events or alarms that are on there. New emails and other messages can also be put on there. It is a way to have all of this at the heart of your desktop. That way, if you see a new one come in, you tackle it right away.

If you want to receive notifications, you can toggle them once you are notified from this. You won't' be able to adjust it until you do so. Now, to add, enable, or disable notifications, click on the action center icon. Press All Settings, and then with the gear icon in the corner, choose the System function in the top left corner of this. Go to the tab that says Notifications and Actions and from there, you will see all of the various apps, and you can toggle as you see fit, such as the tips, reminders, alarms, or even app notifications. You can go to the bottom to enable or disable notifications for various apps in particular. You can even set this up to hide notifications. Remember that to do all of this, you do need to have this installed, and you need to receive one before it shows up.

To dismiss a notification, you simply go to the action center and then move the cursor over the notification you want to go away. Press the X button to the right of this. If you are in tablet mode, you can swipe to make it go away as well, to save you a couple of clicks.

Running Manually Installed Programs

Now, to put programs onto Windows 10 that you want to install, it is actually simple. Just like anything else, you simply insert the disc and follow what it says on the screen. If it does not start automatically, you can browse the disc that it is on to find the setup file, usually under Installe.xe or Setupe.xe and you can open this up.

If it does not start up immediately, you will want to check the AutoPlay settings. To do this, you go to the search box or even the one on the taskbar, and type in AutoPlay Settings and select it to see if it is on. You can choose this for removable drives and memory cards as well.

If you are wondering what you have installed on here, it is simple to find. To do this, you go to the control panel, and from there, you want to type in the program in the box that's located in the upper right area. From there, you can look at Which Programs are installed on Your Computer and look at every single one of them. You can check them, click on them, and then choose to either run them by double clicking it, or right clicking and running it.

For those that do not know how the Windows 10 desktop works, it does help if you do. That way, you can use it to your advantage, and help with various aspects of this as well.

Chapter 5 – Data Storage

Storing data with Windows 10 is actually simple, and there are a few things that you can do with this. It is important to understand how to use the program and file explorer since it can immensely help you. This chapter will work to give you the ins and outs of it.

Program Explorer

Program explorer, or also called file explorer, is where all of your files are located. This includes any documents, applications, or the like on the computer. If you are considering using this type of function in order to store data, then file explorer is the way to go.

One of the best ways to open this is to have it pinned to the taskbar. If it is not already, open up start, type in file explorer, and then right click it so that it's pinned.

Now, the first thing that you will notice is that there are many various documents on here. The first one and the one that can help you the most is Quick Access. This is the default first section of the pane on the left-hand side. Essentially, this is the "bookmarks" bar on this. This shows you the most recently-access folders and the "pinned" folders so that you can manually assign this area to get to anything from Windows. You can do this with virtually anything. You can right-click it, choose "pin to quick access" and once you click on that tab, it's right there waiting for you.

Now with this as well, on the file explorer, you can choose to go to one point or another on this by simply typing in on the search bar what you are looking for.

Storing data in folders

One thing that many people tend to forget when they are using a computer is the ease of storing their data in various folders. Folders make storing this easier, reduces the clutter, and keeps everything neat. If you are going to be sending this to someone, obviously, a folder is the best way to go, and here is how you can store the data that you want into a folder.

First, you want to choose the location for this. This can be either in your documents tab, straight on the desktop, or even on an external device. You can then create a new folder by holding down Ctrl, shift, and the N key all at once. This will then immediately create a new folder in the area, generically named "New folder." Creative, right?

Well from there, you can then rename it. It takes seconds really, but make sure that you type your folder name when it appears first because if you click away from it, it will keep that name until you rename it.

You can also right-click on these by doing the same thing. You should then right click on the blank space where the folder location is located. You should make sure that you do not choose an existing item because it will not give you that. You can choose "New folder" from this menu, where a new one will be created from this.

If you are working with a ribbon menu, you can simply choose "New folder" from the top and it will then create it.

Folders are the best way to store the files and data that you have, and they reduce the instances of clutter on your computer.

Working with files, folders, and external devices

Now, with this, you will probably want to put something in these folders. Well, you are in luck. There is a super easy way to do this.

To add files to a folder, you click on them and then drag them. You can press the Ctrl button in order to highlight multiple things so they are all seen at once before you drag them. Now as of note, if you are putting them in a new location, it will simply copy this, so if you are moving something from Documents to Downloads, it will copy them both there, so you will need to delete the ones highlighted.

But, if you are putting it in a folder, it will move everything to that folder so long as you drag it.

Now, for those of us who have external devices, you will probably want to put something into there. Now before you begin, you will first want to insert the external storage onto there. You'll notice as soon as you do this, you'll see a new menu location pop up, lots of times saying USB device E: or something of the like. Whatever it is, that is your external device.

To move items from your computer itself to an external device, you simply want to highlight what you want to put, and drag it all there.

Now, you can copy and paste this, if that is really, what you want to do. Highlight them, right click and choose to copy, and then open up the tab with the external device on there in order to paste it. It is optional, but it is a choice that you can use.

You want to make sure that once you do that, you press the little arrow next to it, and look for a little green icon on there. From there, you should choose to "safely remote hardware" to remove this. You do this obviously, so that the data is not corrupted.

Copy and moving objects

Now, if you have to say, photos and such, that you want to move around without changing anything, there are a few ways to do this. We will go over the basics surrounding this.

Now, to change the location temporarily, you can use the keyboard keys, and you do not have to change settings. As a rule of thumb, remember the following.

To copy something, press control before you move the file.

To move a file, you want to press the Shift key before you drag it to move it from one location to the other.

If on the off chance you want to make a shortcut to this on the desktop, you simply click on the item and then press the Alt key in order to create this. Then, you can move it. For example, if you want to have the desktop have something automatically shortcutted from where you have it downloaded, you can do this.

You can also change this without using modifier keys as well, simply by going to the Registry Editor and then going to the HIKEY_CLASSES_Root/* key.

From there, you can then create a 32-bit DWORD sort of value here, and this can then determine what data values you want it to have, such as if something should be copied, moved, dragged, or a shortcut.

Now, if you are someone that has many files, the latter might be an easier option. But, if you are someone that only wants to move stuff to a folder, or to copy it, sometimes manually doing it.

To right click a folder, you can then cut or copy it. You can then right click the destination to choose paste. This is something that you do not need a side-by-side window in order to achieve this.

Optical disks you might use

There are a few types of optical discs that you might use. Here are a few of them that you might use and what they do.

The optical disc drive is where the disc is put. Now, there are the occasions where it might not be able to be read, and if that is the case, there are a few steps that you can take.

First, try one and make sure that it is working and not the disc fault.

You should try using My Computer, or from File Explorer. You can try to boot it from there to make sure it is not the drive but the disc.

If you did burn or record something onto an R or RW disk, make sure that it's got playback recording

If you are using this, you should make sure that it is compatible with your computer.

You should be able to use these to troubleshoot the disc if it is not reading.

Working with memory cards and flash Drives in Windows 10

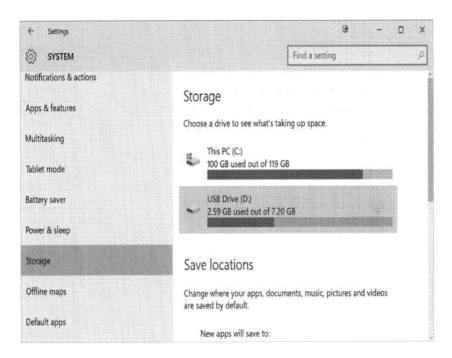

If you are someone that loves to take pictures or videos, chances are that you will have a memory card. You can put this directly into your PC after you move it from the camera. The card has a memory card reader, which is a small box that is plugged into the PC. From here, the PC can read the files, and it does help a lot.

In the same vein, flash drives do the same thing. They are both available at most electronic stores, and you can get these in different variations. You should get the ones that fit your camera before you use it.

The beauty of these is that they are nothing new. The Windows system treats it like an ordinary sort of folder or file on your computer. You put in the card, and then a folder will show up showing the photos on there. The same rules as files still apply, so make sure that you do that. You simply put these in, and you can open both of these with a double click.

Now, as a word of caution, if you format either a card or a flash drive, it will wipe it all out, so make sure you do not care about what is on there.

If you get a message from Windows complaining that the card is not formatted, you will need to right-click, and chose format. The best thing to do in this case is done it whenever you have a new card so that you do not end up taking images that you cannot see and then have to wipe all of this out as a result.

The data storage on Windows 10 is simple, and you can use it with these helpful tips and tricks right here.

Chapter 6 – Reading and Tab management in Windows 10

Another added feature with Windows 10 that you might not know about is reading. Another big part of this is the tab management that has changed with the Edge browser. We did touch on the Edge browser earlier, but this chapter will touch on these, and some of the important factors when you are using Windows 10 and the tabs within.

The Tab management system

Now, before we begin let us discuss a bit about the tabs, and about Edge. Edge is a much faster and much more secure version of the old internet browser that is made for Windows 10, and with the recent creator's update, it is actually faster than chrome and Firefox arguably and often has a much longer battery life. If you are unplugged and using it, you can also stream video and browser for much longer. Edge typically can stream videos for about five hours longer, and you do not even need to stop to charge it, which is good. You can also browse for an hour longer when you are using it, in comparison to Google Chrome, and about two hours longer than Firefox.

One new feature that you can use with this is the setting tabs aside feature, which is located next to the main tabs you have open on Microsoft edge. It allows you to manage all of the tabs quickly that you have looked at. Let us say that you have something you feel like you should keep around. Well now, you can set tabs aside in order to manage everything without losing the overall flow. Instead of having to jump into the whole abyss of trying to find out where that one tab is, you can, when you are at the original tab, just choose to set it aside, and you can then sweep it away, allowing you to come back to it later.

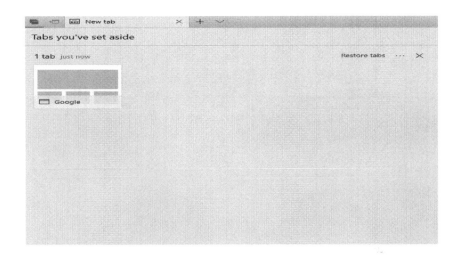

This will also, along with the ones that you've set aside, allow you to preview the thumbnails located on the web pages that you've set aside, allowing for you to restore the collection or singular web pages in order rot pick up where you finished off, allowing for you to have a good idea of where you need to go.

You also can import from another browser. This is super nice because if you've been using the other browsers, and you're ready to move to Edge, you might want all of your favorites back from the browser to edge as well.

Essentially, how you do this, is you go to settings, and then you choose the one that says, "Import from another browser" and then you'll be able to have all of this sent to you.

Finally, there is the jump list. Essentially, you can launch a new window, or an InPrivate window for Microsoft edge directly from the taskbar icon, which allows you to have it in a much quicker manner. You can essentially right click or swipe up, and then choose exactly what you want. It's that simple and truly effective.

Reading on Windows 10

Did you know that you could read books now, similar to how Kindle can on the computer? Well now you can, straight from the Windows store as well, and this new digital category is changing the way that it works. Books allow you to read eBooks from the authors that you love and through various genres, and you will realize that there is a lot here for you to check out, and a lot that this has to offer.

You will find that not only are bestsellers here, but also books from top partners and top publishers as well, and it includes a super extensive catalog of great books in the store in order to help you get started. You can look at various new content, and you will read it straight on the Edge browser itself. It does work offline too, so you don't have to worry about that.

If you're worried about this supporting just online reading, well you don't have to worry, since it is supported by the edge which does do the offline reading. Along with that, you can actually further personalize the reading experience that you have not just with font sizes and themes, but with the way that it's laid out, and even Cortana can bring information from the web in order to enhance your reading experience. Edge also contains integrated learning tools that you can use to help with the reading experience. Edge also has the feature to read aloud as well, and text spacing to help those who have learning disabilities or those who are ESL in order to learn and read better. You can even get them on any sort of machine you want to use, including the 2 in 1 laptops, desktops, and mobile as well. If you're signed in to the same Microsoft account on all devices, it also will hold your place in this as well.

If you are considering listening to books being read to you, I do suggest getting the Dolby Atmos studio experience app that will allow you to have Dolby audio for a Windows 10 PC. You will be able to get this sound directly onto your device, and if you have headphones or even an HDMI connection to a Dolby sound bar or home theater system, it makes it even better. It also works well not just for reading and immersing yourself into this, but overall just the way that you use your PC or other devices with Windows 10 on it.

If you're thinking about trying to learn how to get the most out of your Windows 10 device, you should definitely look at utilizing the edge browser, and the Windows store as well. Both of these have been made even better since the creator's update, so you will get an immersive and very professional sort of system that will help you and allow you to have the best experience that you can have, no matter what device you're on.

Chapter 7 – Managing Programs, Applications and Files

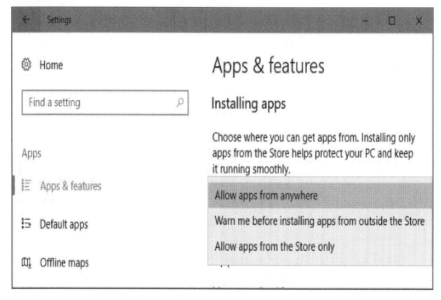

Understanding where your applications and files go on Windows 10 can help you a lot. If you do download and put programs and apps on here, it can certainly help, and this chapter will go over how to put all of this in.

Starting programs and Applications

To start a program or application in Windows 10, it's super simple. In fact, most of you have probably done this to a certain degree already.

To do this, you can choose an app from the startup menu, whether it's via searching, looking at all of your apps, or anything that's pinned to the taskbar. You then click on it, and it will launch shortly after. It's that simple, and in essence, anyone can do it.

All of the programs that you have are available there. If you're struggling with finding that one program that you need, you can always search through the search bar at the bottom, or ask Cortana to do it, and you'll get your answer right away.

Downloading applications from the Online store

So how do you download apps from the online store? This is another super easy one. To do this, you go to the Store icon or type it in on the start menu. It's often pinned to the taskbar. From there, you can sign in with your login details, and you can from there, choose whatever apps you want. You will need to make sure that if you're buying something, you've got a Microsoft account on hand to open it. From there, you can download it, and it'll then be on your computer.

If you don't want to switch to a full Microsoft account, you can do that as well. Simply launch the store from the menu, choose the user icon that you want next to the box, click "Sign in" and then choose "Microsoft account" and then log in like how you normally would. When it says, "make it yours" appears, don't enter your password. You really just want to sign in to use the app instead which in turn will let you use this. It might be a bit lacking, but saves a couple of clicks.

Desktop Shortcuts

Making shortcuts on Windows 10 is actually pretty simple. To do this, you have to just do a few steps.

For apps, you go to the Windows button, then All Apps, and from there, you choose the app, press more, and then press open file location. Once that happens, you right click on the icon of the app and then press Create shortcut. Choose yes, and it'll create a shortcut to the desktop. It's that simple.

Now, for desktop apps, you can create a shortcut by going to the Windows icon, choosing command prompt in the search box below, and then choose command prompt below.

You should then go to the explorer shell: AppsFolder or whatever you want to shortcut. There is a whole list of these. From there you right click the app that you want, choose to create the shortcut, and then select yes. Voila, you've got a shortcut.

Printing and Scanning

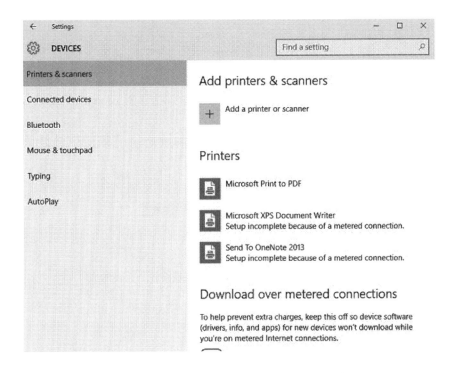

Windows 10 can even help with printing and scanning as well. Here is how you use either.

For printing, it's simple. Make sure that everything is connected, and the software is installed. From there, you can choose a file, or whatever it might be, and you can then press Ctrl+P, which in turn will take you to the print screen. Make sure that the location is the printer that you have, and then, it'll print it.

Now for a scanner, you should first have the scan app installed on this. You should make sure that you have your scanner connected as well, and all pertinent software is installed.

First, you should go find the scan app by either seeing it in the start menu, going to the apps and then from there, you can choose it. If it is saying it's not connected, make sure the USB is connected and you've got the scanner on.

If it's plugged in and also turned on, you'll see the name, and the file type to save these files, usually in the form of PNG. If your scanner isn't recognized by the app, well it's too old then, so you've got to use the old software or get a new scanner.

The scanning app is the easiest one to use.

Now, to change your settings, you should go to the Show More area to figure out if you want to change the color on this, the resolution, where it's saved, and the like. You can mess with these settings as well.

You can then press the Preview button to make sure that everything is correct, and it'll let you preview the scan in the settings that you've chosen. If it doesn't look right, you should make sure that the color mode is chosen. If it's black and white, make sure that it's unlocked, and it can read the material. If the item doesn't fit the entire scanner bed, look for the circle markers and drag them in so that you can surround it.

You can then scan, and when it's finished, press the View button to look at the document.

This chapter went over a few of the great apps that you can get with this, and some of the other neat factors as well.

Chapter 8 – Work on the Internet

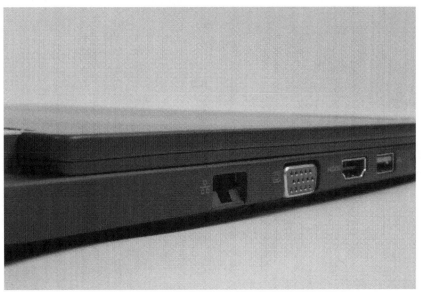

The internet is a great place, and you can use Windows 10 in order to maximize your browsing potential. This chapter will help you with this, and also some of the great implementations that you use.

Connecting to the Internet and Browsing

For those of us that want to use a different default browser, we so can. While Microsoft Edge isn't' too bad for basic stuff, lots of us are so used to Chrome that we don't' want to use something different. Fortunately, there is an easy way to fix this.

First, you want to go to settings, which you can get to simply from the start area. Go to system, and from there, go to default apps, and from there, look at Microsoft Edge. It's down there at the bottom. Toggle the button there to the new browser that you want, whether it be Chrome, Firefox, or Opera if you really use that. From there, you'll notice that the selection is now under that heading.

If you so want to change it again, just come back to this.

Using the Edge browser is okay, but it is lacking. We'll discuss in the next section the pros and cons of the Edge system, and if people actually use this.

For web browsing, you simply type in what you want to find, and voila, you've got it. It's nothing super complex, but it's something that all of us should know.

Should you use Microsoft Edge

Now, should you use Edge? that's the question that all of us have. Let's face it, back when this first came out, it had a lot of bugs, but now, it's got a lot of benefits as well. There are a few things that are great about this, and here is that should be what they are, long with the disadvantages of this.

Speed is something that has been greatly improved. While it might not be perfect, this is one of the deciding factors, since it's actually pretty fast. It's also an app rather than a program, and it sports its own rendering engine. It also can save you space on your hard drive if you don't have a lot of room.

The reading list function is very minimalist, but if you were reading something that you wanted to finish on your laptop, or on your PC, you can sync this up.

In the same vein, there is also the Reading Mode which can be put in, which will take out the extra stuff such as the images, ads, and the sidebars, so it gives you a decent experience.

The reader mode isn't too bad either, and you can use it to tweak the settings as well to make it fit you.

Security is also great on this as well. While IE was awful with that, Edge now provides better, more improved security to help with this.

It also has the annotation mode, which if you annotate, it will show up in OneDrive. One thing of note as well is that these are much more connected.

Now, the biggest disadvantage is that it doesn't have Extension support, which means that it won't' have mainstream adoption, which will cause problems. If you don't want to use extensions, then, by all means, choose Edge, but if you do rely on these, they might not be for you.

The search engines can also be a bit of a pain since it's so different from Chrome and Firefox. It also isn't able to be customized, so there's no way to move the icons around to remove them, and there aren't any advanced features, which can hold you back.

The address bar is also removed as well, so when you open a tab in Edge, but instead it gives you a "Where to Next" area which acts as a search field and address bar.

It also doesn't have the protocol which means that it won't allow you to connect to the site you're active on. The only indicator that shows you that you're connected is the lock in front, so it doesn't have the best security.

Finally, it's messy. It's cluttered, and the menus can look awful, so keep that in mind.

Edge isn't bad, but it's very limited, so make sure that you know this before you go in.

How to Download Stuff on the Web

How you download stuff from the net is insanely simple. If you want to download something, a lot of times, you can click it, and you'll see the file show up in the corner, especially if it's a document file. If you want to do something different with it, you can right-click it.

For pictures, right-clicking and choosing "Save image as" or whatever will allow you to save the image however you so desire. This is a nice feature to have, since all too often if you have file names with just a bunch of numbers on it, this can get quite confusing and not fun to deal with.

Now, you should make sure that if you do download stuff, you know the file is safe. Don't download anything you don't feel like will work for you. If there is a chance for a virus, don't' do it.

Now, if you want to look at the files you've downloaded, you can simply check the download manager at the bottom, or go to the file explorer and look at the downloads folder on your computer.

Social Life: Mail, People, and calendar

Setting a social life factors on Windows 10 is insanely easy, and here is how you do it.

For email, you need a Microsoft account to begin. You want to go to the mail page, add the account, and then you can type in the credentials to get started. Otherwise, at the bottom left of the pan, go to settings, then manage accounts, and then add accounts. You can then choose what kind of account that you want to put in. For google, you'll need to do the two-step verification if you have that enabled. From there, you can then Allow it, and it'll be created.

From Yahoo and iCloud, there might be other steps to do. Most of the time, you should be able to put this in with the simple email address, password, and the account name.

From there, you can press done, and that's all there is to it.

You can then go to the mail app, look it over, swipe to get rid of various parts of it if you do have some files open, and from there, you'll be able to maintain and keep your Windows 10 account up to speed with the email that you have. Your notifications will show up in the notifications center.

For social media, you simply need to have the app installed, and from there, you can then add in your credentials, and the notifications will show up as well.

For the calendar, you want to go to settings as well, add a new one, and you can then add in your Microsoft accounts. If you want to put your google calendar into this, you can't yet, but if you convert it, you can. From there, create it, and you can then either rename your account if it gets confusing or add an event. This will help you get it all sorted out and neatly put there.

Now, as of note, you can use Cortana with this. If you have a microphone and Cortana enabled, you'll be able to use this by simply asking Cortana "Cortana, what are my new emails" or say "Cortana, add ____ to __ at ____" to put in a new event. Your calendar, emails, and the like will be right at your fingertips, and you can do this by simply enabling all of it.

How to Get Permission to Run Software

For some software, it's required to run something with elevated permissions as an administrator. This will allow for more access to various aspects of this, and it will help ensure that programs are run correctly. How do you do this though? Well, you're about to find out.

First, you want to go to the program or the shortcut, and from there, you want to choose to Run as Administrator from the shortcut menu. You will see a warning there, but if you're fine with that, type out the password for this, and then press the Yes button or the Continue button.

For permanent changes, there are a few other steps to follow. Right click the same program, choose properties, click the compatibility tab, and then check mark this to be run as an administrator, and then press Okay. You will need to put the password each time in order to use this.

Windows Defender and the Anti-virus

For those of us that do use our computer to surf the web, you might wonder if you need to get some antivirus software, but in truth, it's actually not the case. In fact, Windows 10 comes with Windows Defender, which is its own anti-virus software.

This is used to keep the PC safe with it built in. It's comprehensive, real-time, and continuous protection from various viruses, spyware, and malware. It's used automatically the minute you install Windows 10. It's used to keep you safe, giving you more of a peace of mind.

This is built in to Microsoft Edge in order to keep you protected when surfing the web. Parental controls, firewall, and even finding your device is enabled here as well.

The best part about this is that it's free.

Now, if you're going to use a third-party sort of browser, it might be best to have some anti-virus software on there as well, but that is optional.

Configuring Parental Control

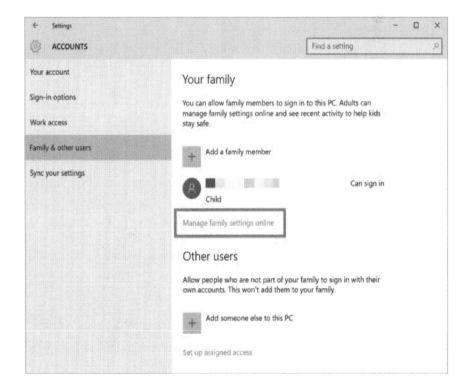

Parents want to make sure that their children are kept safe. It's important to have these parental controls put in, and here are a few to keep in mind.

To check a child's computer activity, you want to sign in to your Microsoft account, and you can then look at all of the accounts and choose the one with the child's name on it. You can then have it report to you anything that they're looking at to give you an active report on what they're looking at. You can also look at the browsing activity and the usage of apps on this page as well, which is another neat thing. You can also block the sites by clicking block to what they're looking at. For this to work, it has to be through Edge so if you are using Chrome, block that too from them.

To adjust the parental control settings, you can then go to each of these settings including web browsing, the apps and games, the purchases, screen time, and the Xbox settings.

For web browsing, you can toggle what should be turned off and on, with it blocking adult content by default.

You can also add URLs if there are extras you want to block.

You can block what they see in certain games and such by blocking adult content or restricting the age of content they can view.

You can also choose the times a child can use the computer, where you can set a start and end time, and if a child gets past that, it will create a popup that will require an adult to log in to continue to use this.

With purchasing, you can review what they bought along with adding money.

Finally, there is the Xbox tab and if your child has one, you can look at the profiles, use video, and see some of the images and what they're sharing online, and also blocking multiplayer games.

With the advent of the internet, Windows 10 has come forward to make web browsing so much easier for you than you could ever imagine.

Chapter 9 – Music, Photos, and Films

For those of us who have media on, our computer putting it on there can be quite nice. If you're wanting to add music, movies, and photos to your Windows 10 device, here's how you do it in a simple, yet effective, manner.

Copying and playing music

Now some of us like to play music, and Windows 10 gives us a chance. Now, there are ways to do this, whether it be through a music app or the like, but really, there are those of us that just really like CDs, and here is how you can copy music from a CD, or even a movie from a DVD on Windows 10, and how you can play it back.

Now first, you want to put the CD or DVD into there, and make sure that it's label-side up. Windows 10 will see it, and you should then look at your choices. You can either Rip the Audio CD, play it, or not do anything.

Obviously, if you want to play it, you should literally choose that, and it'll take you to the Windows media player.

Now, if the notification didn't show up, it's not the end of the world. Go to the desktop, go to file explorer, and then choose the drive below the local disk C. From there, you should then select the manage tab under the area that says Drive tools. You can choose Autoplay here, which will then give you the notification once again. You can then choose the Windows media player.

If you have the settings set up, you can then finish it, and it'll play the music.

To copy, you want to choose Rip CD. This is how you burn it, and if you do this a lot, you can go to the settings and choose "Eject CD after ripping" so that you're not wasting time.

Once this is done, you can then play this by going to the Windows Media Player, choosing whatever song you want, and you can virtually play anything in this app. It's that simple!

Playing movies and TV shows

For many, playing movies and shows is a great feature that Windows 10 offers, and you can watch your favorite program on your laptop.

Now to do this, you need to have the title of the movie or whatever show that you want. From the start menu, there is a movies and TV file there, you should click on it. You can also search for this. You can then click on the movies or TV button on the plane. You can then look at the titles, and click the one you want to put on, whether it is one title, or it is a season of something.

You can then play it, or if you want to, you can download it first, and then use the playback function for it. The same goes for episodes that you can watch as well.

If you want to save space on your drives, you shouldn't download a title unless you really want it and if you're going to be without Wi-Fi for a bit of time, since they do accrue a lot of space.

If you have a video, you can go to the movies and TV file, look for it, and play it. The playback is similar to this as well.

Of course, if you have Netflix or Hulu, you can just download the app and go on your merry way there.

Creating, editing, and saving Playlists

Now, you can create playlists with Windows media player, just by opening it up, selecting "New playlist" and then adding and saving, but the best one for music is the Groove music app. This is something that you can download from the app store.

To add and save the playlists, you first open it up, and on the left-hand side you'll see something called "New playlist" where you can put in a name, and then save this.

Then, you can go to Collection and from there, you can then right click to add a song to whatever playlist you want, and you can add as many as you desire. From there, if you want to change whatever order the songs play, you should hold a song, drag it to where you want, or you can right-click it to remove this to move it up or down.

To remove you simply right click or hold it, and then choose to "remove from playlist" which is located near the bottom area of where the screen is.

Creating a Photo album

The photos app is a great one that you can use. To begin, you should press start, go to photos, and you can then look at everything. It might already be put together, but you can click on each one, and from there, you can choose to move it. or, you can manually move them with your fingers to each respective folder.

To automatically upload photos is to set up automatic upload to the OneDrive cloud from your phone. To do this, you need to install the app on your mobile device, turn on the function of Camera Upload within the settings, and you'll get the latest photos and videos up there. Once they're uploaded, they'll appear in the photos app. From there, you can drag it around and edit the albums to your heart's content.

Media is managed way easier with the Windows 10 system. This chapter talked about how easy it is to do, and how it can dramatically help you with your media sorting.

Chapter 10 – New features and capabilities

In this section, we'll touch upon the new features and abilities of this system, and why Windows 10 is making strides to make this system the best that it can be for anyone who uses it. Here we will highlight the features of each of these.

OneDrive and the "files on demand" system

OneDrive is basically the Microsoft cloud system. It's a great one to have all of the files that you need in your life, right near you at all times.

From this, you can back up, store, and even share with others whatever photos, documents, videos, and even more. Plus, with a Microsoft account, you can get a year of free storage online. It also works with Office online documents, so if you want to share something from OneDrive to PowerPoint or Excel, you totally can. It's the best file storage system for your computer since you can enable this on your computer with just the click of a button.

Fluent Design

If you've ever wanted to design or code an app to how you see fit, you can do it with this.

You can create, code, produce and perform whatever you want, and it's pretty astounding. This is similar in essence to the web kit that you can get with Alexa and Amazon. You can lay it out, style it, control it, design the samples, see how useful it is, and even input it on a device. This is great for those who want to design new and astounding things, and it'll allow you to do so right away.

Windows my People

With the fall creators update, you have something called My People. This is essentially the love child of Skype and the mail system, where if you have contacts that you talk to a lot, and send a bunch of messages to, you can use this to Skype them directly, send messages, and the like. It'll let you know when you've automatically sent a message. Currently, the Skype interface is mostly just a chat interface, but you can do video and voice calls as well. It's still in its formative stages, but it's an app that's coming down the runway and has potential.

Task Manager

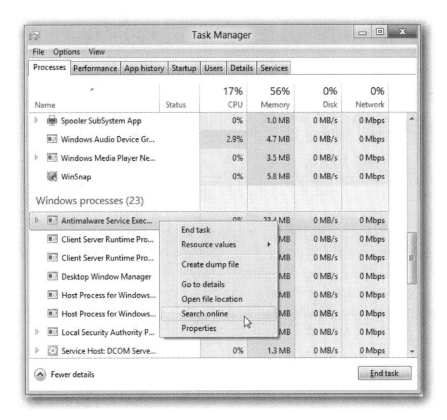

Is your computer running slow? Do you have something that's just totally eating your data? Well, the task manager is perfect for you. by pressing Ctrl+Alt+Del, you will be taken to this screen, where it will show you everything that's using your GPU. From here, you can select various files and programs to close them and force stop, so if you have something that you're trying to get off the screen, but it's not closing, this is how you do it. plus, it can show you any programs that are eating up the speed of your computer.

Windows Story Remix

If you like the photos app, but you want to bring these to life, you can use Windows Story remix in order to do so. It's another beta app that's come out, and from here, you can tweak edits and transitions of various videos and photos that you have, simply by adding 3D effects, various cropping and editing, and the like. You might not have this yet since it's something that's a bit polarizing compared to the photos app, but it will soon be for other various Windows 10 systems once the bugs are taken out of it. You can also add filters, texts, dynamic panning, and 3D objects to any photo.

Spotify and iTunes, keeping your music with you

If you love music, I suggest downloading these apps. They're available in the Microsoft store now, and if you have an account with either, you can access both of these as well. Spotify is great if you have playlists, and if you have iTunes, you can access your personal apple music and videos, along with various apps, and since they work well, you can take all of this on the go.

Power Throttling

If you're someone that notices that Windows is draining your battery cause of background apps, then this is for you. essentially, power throttling is when background work is happening, the Windows system will put the CPU in the most efficient Operating nodes, which in turn showcases that work is getting done and that less battery is spent on work. It actually can save you about 11% on CPU consumption.

Essentially, to control this, you want to control the throttling with the power slider. If you want to opt out individual apps, go to settings, battery usage by app, go to the app itself, then managed by Windows, and uncheck the "reduce work app does in background" to help control what apps will power throttle.

Windows Mixed Reality Controllers

Virtual reality is something that's starting to become more popular, and with Microsoft, they're launching their own version. Windows mixed reality is essentially VR for the Windows 10 system. You can buy the controllers and the headset, and install this on your computer to play some cool virtual reality games.

Currently, it's a bit limited, but with most VR, that is the case. Hopefully, there will be more options soon for this, so that virtual reality can take off.

Installing Ubuntu, openSUSE, and Fedora

You can install all of these onto your system. Essentially, now Windows 10 supports this by adding a "developer mode" to this settings menu of this. You can go to the Windows Store to install any of these systems so simply now with just a click. In the past, it wasn't able to support the other two, only Ubuntu, but Microsoft has been getting lots of requests for them to install this. Microsoft wants to work with the developers in order to make sure that they're getting what they need, so if you're considering programming and development of them, you can use this. It is a bit strange since they're all different shells, it's proving that Microsoft can have these.

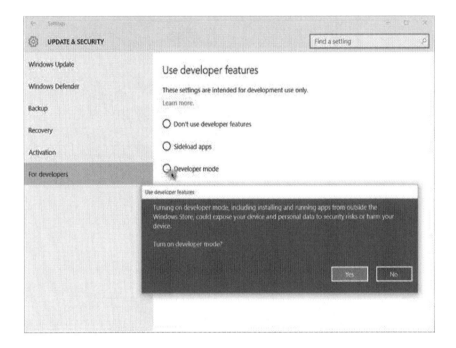

You can go to the Windows store to install any of these.

With these updates, you can take Windows to the next level, using this to better your performance and abilities. For many of us, this can make a world of a difference, and in turn, you'll be able to get the most out of your performance abilities, and the ability of Windows to do what you want it to do, to truly make the best system that you know that you can have. These updates along with the classic system work together to help Windows be the best system yet.

Chapter 11 – Cortana

Cortana is the digital personal assistant offered by Windows—what you can think of as Microsoft's answer to Google's Siri or Amazon's Alexa. It comes fully integrated into this operating system and lets you use voice control on a variety of devices and for an array of helpful functions, both in your main Windows 10 desktop and in programs like Edge.

To set up Cortana for the first time, you want to start by clicking inside the taskbar search box field. The Cortana settings box will appear; toggle the slider on to enable the service. If you need to find these settings later on down the line, you can get to them by clicking on the hamburger menu, then going to "Notebook" and "Settings."

The first time you enable Cortana on your device it will pop up with a privacy statement; you'll have to click "I Agree" before it will let you continue. After you do this, you can enter what name you want Cortana to call you. Next it will ask for access to use your location information. This is recommended to get the most out of the service. The privacy settings app will automatically after you've finished setting up Cortana so you can adjust which other apps have access to your location, as well.

Once you've gone through this process, you'll be ready to start speaking with Cortana. Click inside your taskbar search box and you'll get a display from Cortana telling you she's ready to help you, and prompting you to ask her something. Click on the microphone icon in the bottom right corner of the screen and start speaking.

If she doesn't seem to be able to understand you, you may need to configure your microphone. If you haven't already done this, a box will pop up automatically prompting you to do so. Cortana will give you a phrase that you can repeat to make sure she's hearing you properly. Make sure you're in a relatively quiet place for this step, and also that your microphone is connected and turned on.

Cortana has a host of helpful features that you can explore. You can have her remind you of important dates, or have her set an alarm by saying "Hey Cortana, wake me up at ten AM" (for example). She can also give you news stories based on an array of your favorite topics that you give her as keywords, or alert you when new news reports on your chosen topics are available. She also has a currency converter and a multi-language dictionary for translating and defining words.

If you've given the service access to your location, you can use Cortana to check the weather or inquire about the hours and services of local businesses and restaurants. If you're planning for a vacation, you can also check the weather of other places through Cortana. Simply go into the weather card, click the ellipses, then select "Edit notebook." You'll see an option for adding a city; you can add as many locations as you want. As long as "nearby forecast" is turned on your local information will stay on the top.

Cortana also functions within the Edge browser. You can enable this by navigating to the "Advanced settings" interface, then move the slider to the "on" position next to the option "Have Cortana assist me in Microsoft Edge." Once you've done this, you'll see an "Ask Cortana" icon in the address bar. This icon will animate when Cortana has answers for you.

Changing the language

The default setting for Cortana is English, but she can understand a variety of languages and accents to suit your specific needs. You'll even have the option of recognizing non-native accents, meaning you can use a new language on Cortana to test your knowledge of a foreign language you've been working on learning.

To change Cortana's language, you first need to install the language you want to use. Go to the Windows Settings menu, then navigate to "Time & Language" and click "Region & Language," then "Add a language." A panel will pop up showing you the available language options.

Click the language you want to install. Once it's successfully installed, click on the options to open the settings window. Click on the "Speech" option, then click "Download." You'll need to restart your computer after you've completed this step. After you've re-booted your system, you can go back to "Time & Language," then select "Speech." Under "Speech language," you can choose which one you want to use with Cortana from the drop-down menu.

Composing emails

If you say, "Hey Cortana, write an email" she'll walk you through the steps of composing a new message completely hands-free. She'll ask you who you want to send the email to. You can say the person's actual name or the nickname you've used to save the contact in your address book. If you want to select multiple recipients, just say and between the names.

Once you've added a recipient, Cortana will ask for the subject. After that, she'll move on to the body of the email. If you make a mistake, it's easy to go back and make changes; just say "Make Changes" and tell her where you need to edit, and then continue with your composition.

Tap to launch

You can launch Cortana using a 3-finger tap as well. Make sure you've installed the latest version of the touchpad driver if you want to do this; if you don't, you can download it free from

Synaptics. Go to the "Mouse" option in the control panel then go to the "touchpad" tab, select "settings" and "click" tab, then look for the 3-finger tap option. Cortana will be an option in the drop-down box beside it. Select that, click OK, and restart your computer.

Disabling Cortana

If you decide you'd rather not use Cortana on your device, just click on the hamburger icon and choose Settings. There is a toggle that you can click to disable it. Doing this will also delete all the data Cortana has acquired about the device during its time in service.

Chapter 12 – Adjusting from Windows XP to Windows 10

For some of us, moving from Windows XP to Windows 10 is something that might feel a bit weird. But, while XP is good, it does have a bit of a drawback, since it's got no updates. Windows 10 at first was something many tended to avoid, simply because of the bugs. But, with the fall creator's update, you can now move from Windows XP to Windows 10 without any problems whatsoever. How may you ask? Well, you're about to find out. This chapter will discuss how you can adjust from Windows XP to Windows 10 super easily, and how it's not something to be worried about anymore.

What to Consider

Before you begin moving towards it, there are a few things to consider. XP is something that many people loved, but it's got many drawbacks. However it isn't eligible for the free upgrade, so you'll have to spend a little bit. Of course, though, the cost moving from one to another might be a huge thing to consider.

First of all, think about the lack of security on this, since there aren't any updates to the software or the peripherals being done. Simply put, you're running on an old system.

You will need to back up all of your files before you do end up doing this, since there isn't a way to really keep all of this. It's a bit of a problem, but you definitely should make sure that you have all of your settings and files backed up, and that is definitely a huge part of it.

You should definitely think about the hardware as well, moving everything to SSDs whenever possible. The SSDs do run faster, but it will also cost you in terms of time, and components as well. But, if you haven't moved yet, remember this system is over seven years old at this time, and you should definitely consider moving if you're ready to offset the costs.

You will notice immediately that your computer goes a lot faster when you do install this, and it definitely is a nice thing.

The system requirements haven't changed either, and a clean hard dish means that you don't have to worry about programs slowing down Windows and eating memory as well. It's also pretty light when it comes to the resources that you do need.

Another huge benefit is the security and the compatibility of this as well, but you should make sure that you sync the latest hardware with the software, and Windows 10 will allow you to buy more time with this as well.

Finally, you don't have to worry about the security threat that comes with running an older OS. This will naturally be more secret because it does have built-in antivirus and other protection features too, which is ultimately pretty neat for yourself.

How to Upgrade

There are a few things that you will need before you make the jump to one of these, and we'll discuss that.

First, have a thumb drive that holds minimally 4GB of space, but if you can get more you should do it.

You should also make sure that you have a license code from Windows 7 or 8 since this will help make the jump a lot faster if you're using one machine.

You should have a spare computer that you will be upgrading to. You shouldn't go online with the XP system, so instead, you should use a working machine to help.

You can use a DVD or other way to burn this as well.

Now, you can do this as well with just a disc or download, but sometimes, if you already have the other software, it can make the jump a bit faster.

Now, regardless of whatever version of Windows 10 you decide to upgrade to, you will be able to do this with either a physical disc or a digital download. If you're upgrading straight from XP to the same computer, you should use a physical disc. It is unlikely that an older PC won't have a disc drive, but if you don't have one, you'll need a USB drive

Now, if you are going to a modern computer, you can simply just use the license agreement code, since it can definitely hold that. But, you'll want to make sure that all of the files and folders you want have been copied to either the DVD, the USB drive, or thrown onto a cloud storage service if it has the ability to do so.

Now, you want to take the license keys and the software installation discs. If you don't find them, you can use Magical Jellybean Keyfinder to find the codes, write them down, and then use them.

From there, you should make sure your email inboxes are backed up, and export the bookmarks and settings that they want to keep. You will notice that lots aren't kept, but they should be creating the least amount of pain possible.

From there, you should go to the download page and click on the link for whatever version that you desire. You should only choose the 32-bit if you're using a computer that doesn't include the 64-bit processor. If you're running on an older PC, it might not have it.

Now, you should save the file at this point, and from there create the bootable DVD or the thumb drive. If you do this a lot, you should make sure that you consider getting Windows 10 media as well. You can also speak to the sales rep as well.

You can then go to the setup folder once you've got a bootable drive.

From there, it will then take you to the latest updates, and you should make sure that you do get these since it will bring the creators update to this as well. From there, it will install the latest updates too.

Then, it will look to make sure that the system meets the requirements, and it will then show the "ready to install" area of this.

You might also see a screen telling you that there are a few things that you need to do so that you can install this, and some things holding you back from this.

From there, you will then click the install tab and the PC will reboot.

You will then see the Windows log, along with the language section, making sure that you look at the installer as you reboot and make sure that you don't take out the external drive or DVD. It might automatically do so, but you don't want that. It should automatically happen.

From there, the system will boot, and you'll get asked some questions and from there asked to verify it's you with the ID. At this point, you can set up the structure of what you want on this, and when you finally get to the desktop, it will then search for the drivers. You might see the screen resolution being a bit wrong, but it should then be set after a bit.

Classic Shell

If you really miss the XP look, and you want to bring it back, you totally can. This is something that's been happening for at least six years at this point, and it will let you re-skin the Windows system and change the way the OS looks, along with improving the productivity enhancements, allowing for tweaks to file explorer straight from the start menu.

To do this, you need to install this onto the machine, and from there, right click on the taskbar, choose the settings, and then toggle the small taskbar buttons to on, and then colors, and move it to the blue that's farthest to the left on the third row all the way down. You should make sure the color on the title bar is also enabled.

From there, you can then download the classic shell XP suite and then extract it to the folder that you want to make sure that you have it.

Windows XP is a system that a lot of people do enjoy, and you can upgrade and get the feeling of it once more with your Windows 10 system.

Chapter 13 – The main difference Between Windows 10 and other Windows Versions

So you might wonder if the difference between Windows 10 and other Windows systems is worth it. Well, it is. There are some core differences that end up making it a lot better for you. plus, it is important to understand the difference since a lot of people tend to not realize that this is a huge thing, and while you may not like Windows 10, it does tend to be the best one that's out there when you compare.

Cost Factors

Cost is a huge part of this. now, when you upgrade you're going to have to pay for this at this point, but there are still some ways to get this for free. However, with Windows 7 and 8, they haven't been made free, and they won't ever make them free. Now, Windows 10 is about 119, which might seem like a lot, but the thing is that Windows 7 and 8 aren't getting updates, so your computer is at risk. Do you really want to continue to put your computer at risk when you can just take care of it now by just going to Windows 10, which is better for the system? It probably seems obvious what you need to do here.

Longer Support

Another huge part of this is that support is actually going to be taken away from the Windows 7 and 8 systems soon and that Microsoft won't be supporting this. Windows XP stopped getting support back in 2014, with Vista ending in 2017, 7 in 2020 and 8 in 2023. While that might not seem like a huge deal, you're going to want to upgrade. There aren't new features on the mainstream support when it ends, but they get you with the extended features. That's where Microsoft supports the platform with security features and updates. Windows 10 has five more years of extended support over the other systems, and a lot more over Windows XP and Vista, so you'll definitely want to make sure that you do have this as well.

Universal Apps and flexibility

Now, Microsoft changes the way this works with Windows 10, since with this one, it will allow for all future devices from Microsoft to work on this system, which means that you will be able to run whatever you want on anything, so long as they're connected, which means that one singular app will work in every single place.

It also contains the continuum feature, which will allow for the system to connect either the phone you have or the tablet to the keyboard and monitor, allowing for it to be used similarly to a PC. Windows 10 will be present on every device and the interface it has will work with the environment, be it either the PC, tablet, phone, keyboard, or even the mouse interaction, so you can use all of these singularly in order to have all of this right at your fingertips.

Not so bad requirements

Now, compared to the others, it might not win, but if you think about it, with your PC, you want something that will run the Windows 10 easily, and you'll be able to do this pretty easily. The specifications for the Windows 10 system aren't that much more than Windows 8 and even Windows 7, so it's not like you'll be spending a ton of money in order to do this.

You simply need a gig of RAM for 32 bit, double that for 64, 16 GB for the 32 bit OS, and 20 for the 64 bit, a graphics card that is Direct X 9 or later, and a display of 800x600.

It definitely isn't all that much, especially when you compare it to other systems, and the thing is that it can run smoothly both on tablets and PCs, so it's not like it's super hard to run. It can run on virtually any PC in this day and age, short of the old Windows XP machines. If you do have XP, I suggest upgrading to a newer machine, since that can affect it completely.

Security Settings

Now, Windows 10 wins in this category, and it's a major difference between Windows 10 and the other Windows systems. While 7 and

8 are really good at being secure, Windows 10 takes this to another level, since it will give you even more features. The first is something called "device guard" which will block zero-day attacks by getting all of the unsigned apps and software off. Device Guard can operate in a virtual manner, so even if you have a compromised remote version, you can find the malicious software.

Then there is Windows Hello, which is a support system to reduce the password reliance, simply by using your face, eye, or even the fingerprint. Now, if you don't have the hardware for this, you might not be able to use it, however, it works well, and it does get updates, which in turn will continue with the lifespan of 10 and beyond.

Finally, there are now security patches that are delivered outside of the general updates that will go straight to the machine the moment that they are available. In theory, this means that you're continuously getting the most up-to-date security to your device as well. This will also definitely help with protection as well.

Now, while you might be worried about moving because of the ease of it and the like, it's still a pretty viable system. Windows 10 got a major overhaul with the fall creator's update of October 2017, which added so many amazing new features to the device, and fixed a lot of the major pitfalls.

If you're wondering whether it's for you, look at your current OS. Is it running in a slow, pokey manner to the point where it's just not worth it anymore? Then chances are, it's time for you to make the upgrade it this next-level system, which in turn will allow for a better, more rewarding experience, and in turn, it will allow for you to have the best experience that you can have with Windows 10, no matter where you're coming from.

Chapter 14 – Troubleshooting

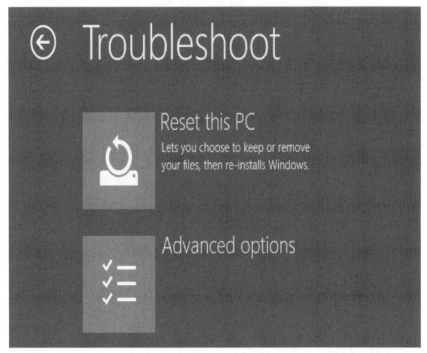

With Windows 10, sometimes there are a few things that you might want to figure out, and sometimes, things can go wrong. Fortunately, there are a few things that you can do in each of these situations, and this chapter will go over the troubleshooting aspects of Windows 10, and how to rectify this situation.

Deleting apps from the system

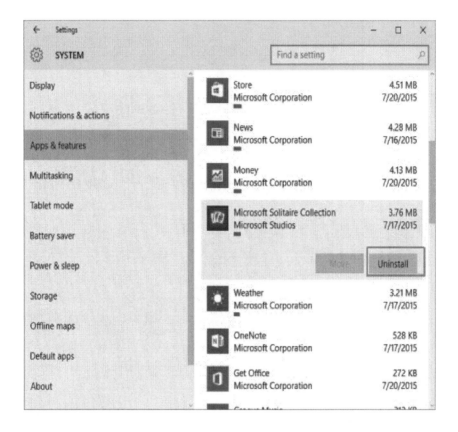

Sometimes your system gets cluttered, and you need to delete some stuff. It's simple though, and here is how.

First, you go to start, and you find the app or program. Right click, and choose to uninstall. From there, you will get a popup window telling you about the dimensions. This might help with space. To finish it, press "uninstall" to complete this.

If it's a program, it might ask you further questions on whether or not you want to uninstall the program. You should click yes, and occasionally there might be an uninstalling wizard to talk to you.

Now, if it's not in the start menu, you go to Settings, Apps & Features, and you'll see all of the programs. To uninstall it, you simply click it, and choose to uninstall. It'll warn you, but if you want to uninstall it, just press yes and uninstall.

Administrator privileges and what they are

Administrator privileges are simple. It basically means who's in charge of the computer and who can make changes. There is usually one who does this, and the rest are guests. If you want to change it, it's relatively simple.

You will want to press the Windows key, and type in cmd at the bottom of this.

Right click on the prompt, and choose to "run as administrator" from the choices. You can also hold Shift and Ctrl in order for you to do this before you start.

You should run the command net that displays all the user accounts. To activate one that's inactive, put in the command net user administrator /active: yes.

If the person is a guest and you want to enable that, you simply do the same thing as above but type in guest instead of administrator.

If you want to password protect it, you can put in a password after this, and type it in once more to confirm it.

Enabling tablet mode

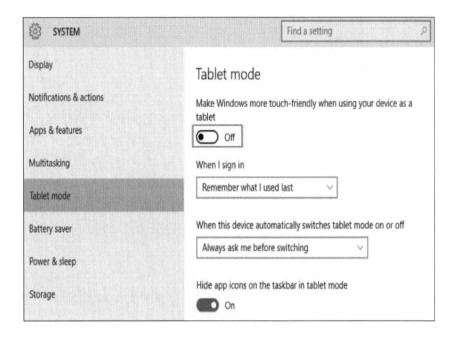

Tablet mode is great if you already have a computer that can work with this. To enable and disable it, you do the following:

First, you go to settings, then system, and then choose tablet mode. You can toggle the first option to enable tablet mode. You can also turn it off to go back to normal.

The third option of "don't ask me to switch" is also something to consider if you want it to switch to whatever one you want without asking you.

Airplane mode

Airplane mode turns off all wireless communications to the device, so you can use it while on an airplane, or to save battery if you're in an area without Wi-Fi or anything. To enable and disable it is simple.

You simply go to the notifications center, and in the area with all the files is an option for airplane mode. Toggle it on or off to change this.

Changing the orientation of the screen

Sometimes you want to rotate the scene on something. To do this, you should press Ctrl+Alt+whatever arrow key you want to press. The arrow will determine the screen direction. If it's on tablet mode, it'll happen automatically. This is useful if you want to fill the screen while it's on its side, so you can flip your monitor on the side to get the right resolution.

Data recovery and how to do it

Sometimes you got to do a sweep of the files, and the best way to make sure that you do this is to use file history. This is the best way to restore the various built-in system in order to recover this.

Now, to get this, you should open up the folder with the deleted file. You can then go to file history and see everything. You can then choose the one you want to retrieve, and then press Restore to get this back.

If the file history won't help, you can locate it by using data recovery software, and press Scan to find these files. You'll see them come up, and after that, you can choose this by pressing Recover to get them back. You can save your recovered files then to a different drive to prevent the recovery failure of this.

How to restore Windows 10

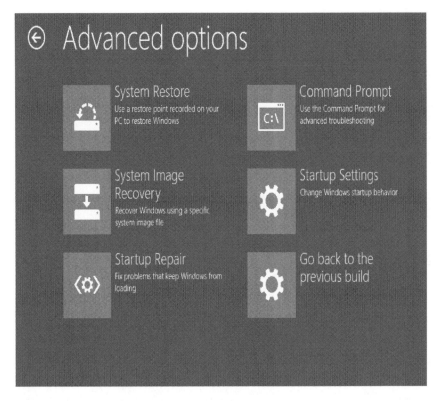

Sometimes you got to fully restore Windows 10. Here is how you can do it. First, you go to settings and then choose Update & Security. Press Recovery, from there, you want to choose to reset this PC, go to an earlier build, or Advanced startup.

Resetting this will start fresh, advanced will let you boot the recovery drive, and "Go to an earlier build" is good for those that want to use an earlier OS.

You can reset the PC, and then you're given the option to either keep the files or remove everything. Regardless, the settings will default and the apps will be uninstalled.

If you're giving the computer away, it's advisable to remove everything, since the person won't be able to recover the erased files. If it's going to you but you want to make a clean sweep, just choose to remove the files.

Finally, press Next, Reset and continue to fully finish rebooting this.

Common error messages to watch out for

Sometimes you see some common error messages, and here are some you should watch out for.

Battery low: this means you need to charge it.

Windows update error 0x80070057: this is an installation error when a backup fails, or when updates aren't installed. Typically, you need to rename the folder, edit a few files, and manually replace the corrupted ones.

DLL Error: this is a shared file that some programs use for action. These are built in and essentially are like test pages. If it says it's missing, you should check for driver updates and do fix them.

Certificate security errors: this is something that's there to keep you securely connected to whatever sire of choice, and shows the legitimacy of it. To fix this, adjust the date and time and synch it. If it's still wrong, you might have to replace the motherboard.

Blue screen errors: these are the most famous, and it means there is a problem that Windows can't fix. To fix this, look at the code and see if it's a bad driver, a defective ram, a bad hard drive, or if you need a reboot.

Technical support

There is a small technical support line. If you want to get into a snag where there is a question, simply press the "help" button or type in help in the start menu. This, in turn, will allow you to search for the various questions you might have, and you can find the answers there. This is the cheapest way to go.

Paid technical support from Microsoft

If your problem is way more extensive, you might need to get paid support from Microsoft. This is about 99-149 dollars and they're designed to be small sessions to get rid of Malware, speed up your computer, and also help to solve problems with this.

This appears in the Microsoft store, and you can simply choose this, and you'll be able to get the answers that you need.

I don't suggest going to this unless you're really pressed for solutions, but if you run into bugs with this, you can always contact Microsoft to better help you with this situation.

Free technical support from Microsoft.

The Answer Desk is the free answer support system that you need. This can help you with the following:

- Diagnostics on your device

- Software repair and help

- Virus and malware help

- PC tune-ups to make performance better

- Recycle for rewards

- General help questions

This is something that you can go to if you have questions about your account, apps and the like. It also works for mobile devices and Xbox as well.

This might be where you go if you can't get answers from the Help tab on your device.

Sometimes bugs happen, and if you're able to get the help that you need to improve the system and the like, you can always go to the help line for help. You deserve to have a good, running PC, and this, in turn, will help you.

Chapter 15 – How to Improve Your Windows 10 Experience

So what are some ways to improve your Windows 10 experience? Well, we're going to go over a few of the major ones that you should consider if you're going to be doing the upgrade, how they can affect you, and some helpful screenshots to assist you in this. This chapter will dedicate itself to that so that you have a better idea of just what it is that you're getting into.

Eliminating Blue Light

One thing that some people like to turn off on their laptop or computer itself, is the blue light. The blue light from bright screens can actually reduce the chances for us to fall asleep, and if you leave your computer on, it could end up affecting you after you're done. It's something that can throw off the circadian rhythm, and it's a feature that many don't consider, but it can be a problem.

However, Windows 10 includes a nightlight, and we'll discuss how you can get to there.

First, you open up the menu at the start. You should then select the little gear sign, as highlighted in the screenshot.

At this point, you'll be taken to settings, which is where you want to go. You want to go to system, then display, and then move the switch for the night light to on.

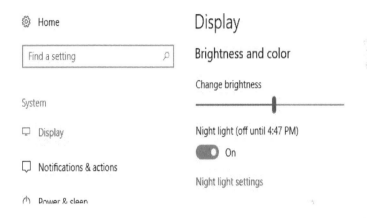

You can as well at this point change the settings for night light too, including the brightness, and you can change the brightness automatically when the lighting changes. You simply do this by going into the settings tab on this and choosing it for your device.

Synching your iPhone

For some of us users, you want to synch up your iPhone to your device. There are a few things that you can do in order to accomplish this, and this chapter will discuss how you can synch up your phone to your Windows 10 PC

First, you want to connect your phone to your laptop using the cable that comes with it. From there, the computer will ask for phone access, so you can click continues so that it gets this.

With an iPhone and iTunes, it will automatically show the library, so if you don't have your iPhone already synched up with iTunes on this, do so now.

You will want to press the phone icon, and then the button that says to sync. You should be able to sync up the two devices. From there, if it doesn't happen, you should go to the sidebar, and from there, press the synch checkboxes that are present under the apps, movies, and music tab, and then try to synch up once again.

This could end up taking a while, especially if you're synching up a lot, so you can grab a snack or do something for a few minutes while it's synching.

When it's finished, you want to check the phone, apps, videos, and music, checking to make sure they ended up on the phone.

Connecting Bluetooth to the device

For some of us, we want to use our computer and phone to Bluetooth share. There is a simple way for you to do this, and you can do so with Windows 10.

To begin, you want to put the device in, and make sure that it's set up as well with Bluetooth. You can from there go to settings, turn on the Bluetooth, and then make sure that it's on. You can then connect the devices together.

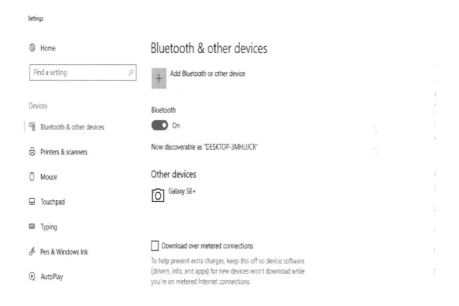

It's that simple, regardless of if you're using an iPhone or Android device.

Shrinking Windows 10

One thing you might notice is that Windows 10 is taking up a lot of your space on your device. If you find that it's creating this problem, you're not alone. It tends to be a bigger system, and it's hard to truly shrink it, but there are a few ways for you to do so.

The first is that you can uninstall the default Windows 10 apps. There are a few that come pre-installed when you install Windows 10 on your device. They don't take a whole lot of space on an individual sense, but over time, they do tend to clutter. I do suggest uninstalling the ones that you feel you don't need.

To do this, you go to settings, settings, system storage, apps & features, and then choose the ones that you want to install in order to uninstall them.

As you can see from the screenshot here, there are some apps that you can get rid of, and if you choose to uninstall them, you can simply do so. It's that simple, and for many people, it can be a big thing.

Turning off Hibernation

When you turn on hibernation mode, it will keep it in the same state until you turn it back on. If you don't use it, it might be best to uninstall it. You can disable and get rid of it, and this actually can give you a few gigs of space.

To do this, you want to right click on the Windows start button and choose the one that says command prompt, admin.

You can then open it, and then type in the following: powercfg-h off, and then press enter.

This, in turn, will delete the file and reduce the option to hibernate the system. You can still put it to sleep, and the computer will put the state to the memory instead of the hard drive, keeping it on but reducing the power of it.

Deleting the old Windows Folder

If you have a computer that was recently upgraded from Windows 7 or 8 to 10, then awesome. But, you may not know this, but what's not so awesome, is that Windows 10 likes to keep a copy of it on there. This might not seem like a big deal, but it's actually a huge file, about 15 GB of wasted space on the device. Did you know that there is a simple way to get rid of this? That's right, you can get rid of this in a couple of different ways, and we'll also show you a couple of neat little features that this involves as well.

First, you want to type in something called "free up disc space" into the Windows search box. You want to then click on the shortcut that says this.

From there, you can then click OK and change the drive if you have the Windows disk not already chosen. You can then choose to clean up the system files. From there press OK when you see the drive letter displayed once again, and you'll then notice the disk cleanup window will show up again.

You can then check the previews Windows installation in the files area and then choose OK. You can then delete these files, choose yes once asked again, and then you'll then be asked to have wait as it deletes this. This should take maybe about 30 or so seconds.

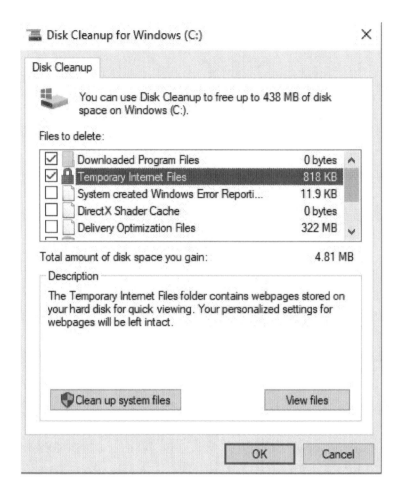

As of note, it is important as well to consider deleting some of the temporary internet files as well and some of the temporary files as well on your computer. This, in turn, will help speed up your computer, and also give your computer a lot more space as well.

Cleaning the WinSxS Folder

Another storage space that you need to consider is looking at the WinSxS folder, which is used to store the files that you will need for the installation, along with backups. This is another huge space hog on your computer. If you're running out of space, or you want to speed up your computer, you should make sure that you do so. This will also cause the computer to hold onto this with each update, which isn't good at all.

Now, you can't delete everything, because some are needed for Windows to run in a reliable manner. You can use the command prompt to clean up the file as well.

Now, you'll want to go to the Windows update cleanup, and from there, choose the OK button.

If you don't see the update cleaning option when it comes to disc cleanup, there isn't anything which can be deleted in a safe manner. You can also do this with the command prompt as well, but it's a whole lot more work, and it might not be as easy to navigate as the other options might be.

When it comes to improving your computer and making your machine the best that it can be, you need to start looking at different ways to both speed this up, and make it as efficient as possible. Luckily, this chapter discussed a few surefire ways to help with improving the system, allowing for a better, much more rewarding experience when it comes to improving the Windows 10 device that you have.

Chapter 16 – Other Tips and Tricks

Windows 10 is a comprehensive and complex operating system, with a lot of different onboard features that will be useful for different groups of people. Even if you're relatively comfortable with most aspects of the Windows 10 interface, scanning through the different options in this chapter can help you to deepen your knowledge of your operating system, and may make you hip to some features and options you didn't realize were there.

Developer mode

In previous versions of Windows, you needed to have a developer's license to develop, test, or install apps that weren't officially approved by Microsoft. This is no longer the case in Windows 10. Anyone can enable the developer mode on this new operating system. Most regular users won't need it for anything, but it does have one extremely useful purpose: side-loading apps.

Side-loading means installing an app that is not available through your device's usual store—in this case, one that you can't find in the Windows store. Once you're in this mode, you can download and install any app that you find online that is compatible with Windows. You can even install UWP apps that aren't signed, an option that was difficult to activate on previous versions of the operating system.

You can activate Developer Mode by going into the Settings, then into "Update & Security" followed by "For Developers." You'll see Developer Mode as one of the options. You can activate this on any version of Windows, even the ones for home use.

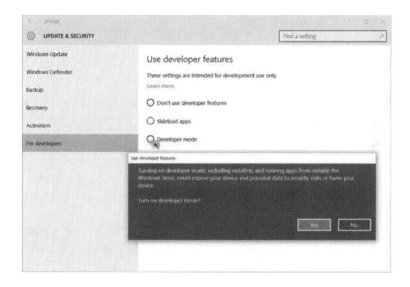

Once you've installed a side-loaded app, it's a good idea to debug it, as well. You can do this in the Visual Studio once you've enabled developer mode. This is an excellent option for people who make their own apps, as well, letting you make sure your app will function correctly before you upload it for others to download.

Putting your operating system in developer mode will alter other aspects of your system as well. It lets you quickly change a whole host of system settings so that they're better for developers. It also will show file extensions, empty drives, system files, and hidden files, all things that are typically hidden when you're not in this mode. When you look at the file manager's title bar, you'll see the full path to a given directory; you'll also be given easier access to the option to run as a different user.

Keyboard shortcuts

If you're still primarily a keyboard and mouse navigator, keyboard shortcuts can be incredibly helpful, letting you work more quickly and efficiently than clicking through a bunch of menus. Windows 10 still uses the familiar shortcuts that were available on previous Microsoft products, including Ctrl+C for copy, Ctrl+V for paste, and Ctrl+A to select all on a page.

There are some established shortcuts that are less well-known but can be equally helpful. If you hold Shift while you drag something to the Recycle Bin, for example, it will be deleted instantly. If you hold Ctrl+Shift while you're dragging a folder or icon to a new destination, it will instead create a shortcut.

You can also easily access the various options and commands in Windows using keyboard shortcut. If you hold Alt while you click on a file or a folder, it will open the properties box, which will give you a variety of different options for interacting with the program. If you hold the Windows key along with X and A at the same time, you can open the elevated command prompt on the desktop, which doubles your options over the typical context menu.

There are also some new keyboard shortcuts that have been introduced as of Windows 10 and utilize the Windows key (or

WinKey, for short). Many of these are for navigation. Win+T cycles through the apps that are open on the taskbar. Win+M minimizes all windows, switching you to the desktop, while Win+D switches you to "Show Desktop." If you press the Windows key along with a number, it will switch to that numbered application in the task bar. Holding the windows key while tapping the plus or minus keys will zoom you in and out, respectively.

Other new keyboard shortcuts are for opening useful applications. Win+Tab opens Task View, and Win+A opens the Action Center. Win+E launches the File Explorer; Win+I opens the Settings app. You can also press Win+Alt+D to open up the date and time.

There are also some keyboard shortcuts for use specifically with Cortana. To launch Cortana, hit Win+S; to launch it in listening model, hit Win+C. You can also press Win+Shift+C to open Cortana after it's been launched.

If you want to lock the orientation of the screen, you can hit Win+O. This will mostly be of use to mobile users, but can also be used with laptops that have a flippable screen. You can also hit Win+L to send the device to the lock screen manually rather than waiting for it to time out.

Mouse tips

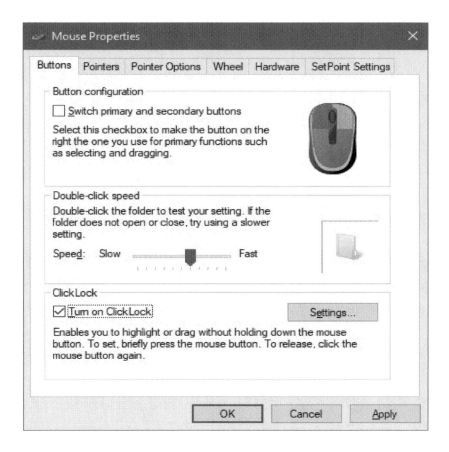

Along with the keyboard shortcuts, there are a variety of tricks for using your mouse that many users aren't aware of. For example, if you hold the Shift key when you click, you won't have to hold down the mouse button to select text. This is also an easier way to select partial words if you need to do so.

Holding Ctrl while you select things lets you select multiple pieces of text at the same time. If you want to select a vertical swath of text, you can do so by holding Alt while you click and drag. These selection tools are less likely to be useful for most users, but may come in handy depending on your purpose.

You can also use your mouse to do some other things you may not have thought of. If you want to open multiple links at once, you can do so by holding Ctrl while you click on the links you want. Holding Ctrl while you're clicking on a single link will open it in a new tab. You can also get an extended context menu on by holding Shift before you right click.

Desktop shortcuts to settings

Creating a shortcut for a program or app is as easy as right clicking on the desktop and selecting "New" and "Shortcut." If you want to create a shortcut to a particular, oft-used setting, though, you'll have to go through a bit more of a process.

The first thing you'll need is the Uniform Resource Identifier for the setting, also called the URI. This is a string of characters that stands in for a particular setting. Microsoft has a webpage that lists all of the URIs for the settings in Windows 10 (https://msdn.microsoft.com/en-us/library/windows/apps/xaml/dn741261.aspx).

Once you've located the URI for the setting you want to make a shortcut to, you can follow the steps above for creating other shortcuts. Type the URI into the wizard that opens when prompted, then name the shortcut. If you want to change the icon, you can do so by right clicking on the shortcut then clicking on "Properties" followed by "Web document" and "Change icon."

Moving the taskbar

The default, familiar location for the taskbar is along the bottom of the screen, and for most people this is the most comfortable place for it to be. You might not realize, however, that this isn't your only option. If you want to position the taskbar elsewhere on your screen, just right click on it and uncheck the "lock taskbar" option. You can now drag and drop it to the top or sides of the screen.

Shut-down through Cortana

There are a lot of useful things that you can have Cortana do without any extra steps or tweaking, but when you first load her up she won't be able to trigger shutting down, restarting, or logging off of your computer. You can get around this by creating a shortcut to the function, then asking her to open it.

Start by opening your file explorer and navigating to C:\<username>\AppData\Roaming\Microsoft\Windows\Start Menu\Programs. Once you're in this folder, create a file shortcut by right clicking then selecting "New Shortcut."

A location field will appear. What you type in it will depend on what you want Cortana to do. For shutting the computer down, type "shutdown.exe −s" if you want to have her trigger it immediately, or "shutdown.exe −s −t" followed by a number of seconds if you want it to leave a slight delay. If you want to restart, type "shutdown.exe −r"; for logging off, it's "shutdown.exe −L".

Name the shortcut with something that you'll remember easily for the function you're using. Once you've created this shortcut, you can have Cortana use it by saying "Hey Cortana, open" followed by the shortcut's name. Your computer will then perform the corresponding action.

Recycle bin tips

Everyone is familiar with the recycle bin on their desktop, but you may not be aware that you can customize it, as well. If you right click on the icon and select "Properties," you can adjust things like the maximum size of the bin or the icon that represents it. You can even set it to automatically permanently delete anything that you put in it if you don't want the intermediary step of putting it into the recycle bin.

If you accidentally send something to the recycle bin, you can restore it by opening the folder of the bin, right clicking on the item, and clicking "Restore." Conversely, if you want to permanently delete a single file, you can choose "Delete" from the context menu that opens when you right click.

Notepad tips

One program that's on every Windows computer but is often neglected by the majority of the users is the Notepad. This is a very simple text editor that can be extremely useful for smaller documents or simple typing, and it has a broader functionality than you may realize.

When you're inside Notepad, you can press F5 to add a date and timestamp. If you want a timestamp to appear every time you edit it, you can type .LOG in the first line of the file and this will generate automatically. There are also keyboard shortcuts you can use to add the date or time: &d (for the date) or &t (for the time).

The ampersand generally comes before all the keyboard shortcuts in Notepad. Others include &f to print the name of the document and &p for the page number. If you want to align the text, use &l (left), &c (center), or &r (right).

Finally, there is some customization you can do to the interface using the menus on the toolbar along the top of the screen. The font is a very simple one by default but you can change it in the "Format" menu. If you open the "File" menu, you can use the "Page Setup" option to customize the document's orientation, margins, and general size.

Paint tips

Another oft-neglected program is Microsoft Paint. It is a simple photo editor, in some ways the image equivalent of the Notepad text editor. While it certainly won't give you the seamless photo editing of Photoshop or similar programs, it still has its uses.

One thing that paint does easily is let you invert colors, something that a lot of users don't realize. You can also change the style and size of the brush, either through the menu on the top toolbar or by using the keyboard shortcut of holding the control key while you tap the plus or minus buttons. This trick works for the pencil, eraser, and spray tools as well.

There is also an easy way to use Paint as a color replacement tool using the eraser. Put the color you want to replace in the first swatch space, then put the new color in the second swatch space. If you wave the eraser across the image while holding down the right click button, it will replace the first color with the second.

You can even use Paint to create your own gradient. Do this by opening a blank image, putting a diagonal line across it, then filling each half with a different color. Go to the "Resize" tab and edit the horizontal value to 1, then uncheck the "aspect ratio" box and close the dialogue box. Now re-open it and change the horizontal value to 500. Do this a few times; the two colors will be blended into each other in a gradient style.

Conclusion

From this, you can see here that Windows 10 is making strides in the realm of bettering the performance of your PC. It is still getting there, but with the recent Fall Creator's update, now systems and features have been unlocked, and new various settings have started to come forward as well. With this, you can see from here just what the potential of Windows 10 is, what it has to offer, and the like. You'd be amazed at the difference it makes to use this system when compared to others that are out there.

The next step that you should obviously take, is to start focusing on how to implement this into your life. The best thing is to get the Windows 10 system, and put it on your computer if you haven't already. This is a guide not just for those that want to take it to the next level, but for those who have never ever used a computer in such an in-depth manner before. With this as well, you'll be able to truly choose for yourself what you want out of your computer system, and from there, you'd be amazed at the difference that this makes. You'll be able to truly make it so that you're able to have the best and most efficient Windows 10 system out there, and from there, you can use it in order to build a better system, make your life easier, and use this great software to make your life much more efficient.

I hope, that you really enjoyed reading my book.

Thanks for buying the book anyway!